TOM MAC INTYRE

Stories of the
Wandering Moon

THE LILLIPUT PRESS
DUBLIN

First published 2000 by
THE LILLIPUT PRESS LTD
62-63 Sitric Road, Arbour Hill, Dublin 7, Ireland.
www.lilliputpress.ie 24/5/01

10 9 8 7 6 5 4 3 2 1

A CIP record for this title is available
from The British Library.

ISBN 1 901866 48 3

*The Lilliput Press receives financial assistance from
An Chomhairle Ealaíon / The Arts Council of Ireland*

Acknowledgment is due to the editors of Books Ireland and Krino,
where some of these poems first appeared.

Set in Monotype Centaur
Printed in Ireland by Betaprint of Clonshaugh, Dublin

Contents

Drawings on pages 2, 28 and 46 by Barrie Cooke

PART ONE

Interview

'What was the hardest
ever shot you
had to stop?'

'It was from
a woman. No cover
that day. She
waltzed clean through.
Out I come
to meet her.
(*Hold it just
there.*) One on
one, a lot
in a look. (*Now
let her roll.*)

Open Door

Year-round open season
in that cacophonous café:
across a vapoured month
of wet Sundays she'd
fixed me down the barrel
of her lassitude, dearth,
perfervid sang-froid – 'For
whom are you saving it?'

The venue slid. The house
now, the stare's mitigated.
She looks about, curious,
wanders the odd smile,
stipples grace-notes
of distress. 'Why's it
you always send me away?'
Difficile à dire, ma belle.

In the no-prisoners-taken
of the small hours,
a cough in the next room,
coughing reverberant,
farouche, lenitive. Hold yet,
let it wrap you again.

'Been there long?' 'About
an hour.' Triumphantly culprit
her demeanour, aspirant
gamine. She cleared
her throat. *Au lit.*

Vertigo

That sleepless
abundant
neglected
ora pro nobis
heather-pink:

colour of your
labia exactly as
your lipstick —

for a moment,
call it years,
I'd no notion
where to look.

Beauty Spot

Butter-blonde — 'True
we have lots more
fun,' she'd venture,
ache the undertow.
Smelled of basil.
Big bothered hands,
her touch, that dulcet
touch another planet.
Complexion — pale
by winter, high summer
sonorous peaches-and-cream.

In one eye —
darkling —
a fleck of hurt,
kindergarten accident.
Wakeful beauty spot,
you couldn't miss it,
well, you could. Some
did. Meet it, ever
ever after it must
sing her home.

Guess

Which eye was that
talisman of hurt?
So. He's forgotten,
who knew those eyes
better than his own.
Call up her face.
Tried that, mate,
got me nowhere,
beg leave to guess.
Has it come to this?
Leave given to guess.
The left eye, left.
Left. Sure of that?
Wait a minute. Let
it swim close. Come
close, love, closer ...

Can see it now.
Salut. The left.
Would be the left.

Fabulous

My father, by the way,
isn't really my father,
he lives overseas —
the real one, I mean,
met him once — almost,
I somehow managed
an eventful non-
meeting with my absent
father who designates
me a non-person —

distressful lids brush
the emphases, flit,
find an isthmus
for a princess fit —

sixteen, never been
anything'd, get myself to
fair Copenhagen,
this restaurant where,
I learn, my loving father
nightly wines and dines.
All right, quiet corner,
place crowded, 'bout
ten o'clock, I'm at
the coffee stage, count-
ing losses, when in
he strolls, pampered latest
on a pampered arm. Dead
spit of me as

I'd known to expect. The man
transmits, I thought —

a sigh — no — not yet —

I watch, I don't watch,
they're seated, the pair,
I summon the moment —
obedient, it arrives,
our eyes meet, his
a bold turquoise blue,
everything stops, every-
thing continues, who
cares, we'd touched,
scorched, tell the sweet truth
we'd sort of fucked,
me — I'm totalled —

lowered lashes you'd
risk limbs to kiss;
an enlightened pallor —
swiftly roused —
makes its case,
narrator comes to
healthily on cue —

was I the subject of
a quick faint — trance —
wish I knew, any-
way, when I regain
poor orphaned wits,
he's gone, she's gone,

five minutes passed
on some clock, a waiter
appears, and — still
don't quite believe this —
dinner on the house
is alluded lightly to ...

O my seanachie born,
you could sing it
you do you do
more of your story
tell me tell me
more of your story
for Johnny Magory ...

The Cry

The cry rose, tangled
her breath, found a way,
bawled, sobbed, wept,
whimpered, whinged,
faltered, resumed,
louder, wilder ...

Shameless, bidden,
she became her tears,
let the flood take
what course it would,
she glistened, shone,
gathered light until,
this side *Amen,*
I could not tell
ma belle from waterfall.

She looks up, contrite,
streaked, biting
an unruly lip: reach,
hold close, comfort,
lumpish welcome her
from The Land Under Wave.

Fingertips

Touch me, Mister.
You're touching me
differently, aren't you?
Do that again, please –
that's it exactly –
you've moved to meet
your far fingertips –
don't I'll start over –
write about it now
you know about it –
'There's a water-drop
in every fingertip,' cried
The King's Daughter,
'touch me with those.'
Told you I'd start over –
be weeks, months, late –
for what? – everything –
you've dolphin hands
were you born
near the sea
your fingers are
stranger than anyone's

Promenade

To look – or look away –
you are compelled,
privileged to expand
a wonder story.

Our table's spread,
verily, it groaneth.
So it is, we
surface rarely,
bit dishevelled
(please excuse us),
always in repose.

Daughter

This glade is home
and time to learn.
My father's here,
dead and coffined,
also beside me —
figure of power.

Check his coffin.
A box on the lid,
in the box I find
a child's night things,
pillow, coverlet.

'One who's not aflame',
he says, 'can't burn.'

The Carpenter's Daughter

Well, since you ask the question,
she was the carpenter's daughter
fair. The father's workshop surely
figured. Abundant coffins,
spirit-levels that sang clear,
peachy fuzz of the sawdust,
and, glory of the *mise en scène*,
wood shavings to the knee —
odorous, innocent, unregenerate
flux, out of which stepped
Celia, black hair *flagrante*, com-
plexion an unlikely, thrilling,
prelapsarian *café au lait*.

Would she like to play Doctor?
The chosen didn't have to be led,
gave — *soignée* — the mortal nod.

We made, at speed, for my abode,
detached, spacious, somnolent.
I take her to a neat west-
ward facing room known as —
a former occupant's profession —
'The Surgery'. *Gaudeamus.*

The game of 'Doctor', for two
concerned practitioners, organ-
ises itself at a supple lick.
A table, large, is covered
by an expansive rug — or rugs:

let rug — or rugs — hang,
all sides, to the assistant
floor. Pause. Admire the work.

No one knows where we are.
No one guesses our mission.
We enter our well of shadows.
Celia reclines. And is bare
to the waist, no least action
required on her part — or mine.

We are both
unconscionably calm.
Her thighs muse in the dusk.
My gaze opens
to the wink between.
Now it comes:
an odour, odours,
odours of Celia
Celia adorning.

Mom Speaking

Her mother's on the phone.
'Ma belle's a good girl,'
she tells me over again
as though I'm somehow simple.
I agree to the proposition –
ma belle's a good girl.

Her mother has a theme –
variations will be minute;
'Ma belle is warm,
ma belle is brave,
ma belle has a gift.'
I agree, I agree, I agree.

Her mother's voice comes
from a place far away,
it proffers concern
and an intimate remove,
it owns the courtesies,
will not speak out of turn.

Her mother's voice dips low –
'Ma belle can be headstrong,'
she is entering a plea,
'Ma belle can be wild,
ma belle is, after all, young …'
Do I understand? I understand.

Her mother reads my thought.
We lean on the quotidian –

the usual reliable topics
find us immutably at one.
'Good talking to you then.'
Her mother's off the phone.

Billet-doux

Your love-sounds
Mister Honey are
tropical birds

a slow air
blown south
filtered by leaves

transparent as cellos
fresh from the vat
of last year's laughter

palette's wet
blue avocado
travelled gamboge

simple credo
'the concert's now
or just before'

(phone me when
you get in
love ye ciao)

Waiting

Timid with hunger,
bit of a ghost
from your summer
in that vestibule.

Tomorrow we'll visit
the settling grave.
Today? We've the wit
to hold till night.

So: eye each other,
swop words, stories,
come morning share
a tousled wreath.

Bronze Fennel

I never see bronze
fennel in the spring
but your pubic fuzz
shamelessly gives tongue,

flicks us both
to a garden clear
where, drunk and sober,
we transform to
herbaceous border,

well-drained, loamy
soil, sun, faint
aniseed (is it?) breath,
liquorice the under-glow.

The garden's aware,
the garden's unaware,
the garden is
the sudden-summer
pheromonal honey-flow …

Afterwards, we sprawl,
number echoes,
vanish by-and-by.

Hold-all

The bag you carried
when we first got together ...

I've watched that bag
crimp, gather quiet,
shift, sudden as soot.

I could take you to see it —
asleep in a cupboard,
caught in a sun-trap,
looking out of a tree,
the brink of a smile.

Pillow-Talk

We swop dreams
if we remember,
last night he dreams
his one daughter,
in the dream she's
twelve, thirteen, an'
doin' a dance
with flowers, weeds —
he knows it's her
Ophelia send-up,
they laugh together,

next two birds,
sea-birds, become
two flat-fish
(I'm Pisces, *en passant*),
John, he says, Dorys,
there on the sand,
edge of the water.

What's that all about?
'The bejaysus factor
in the distant blue.'
I stretch the pause.
'Take me this time
par le petit trou.'

Immersion

Long enough inland
we hit the shore,
your patch. The sundown
favours an old friend,
you hum destination.

Shrug: garments gone.
From her element,
she rises, dripping,
arms out, legs wide,
cunt – pellucid.

I breathe my last
will, timid testament –
'Scatter everything here' –
stumble to dare
our lap of flood-tide.

Blaze

Returned to the world,
enquired had she
noticed anything out
of the way – 'Thought',
the syllable curled,
'something strange goin'
on down there' –

the meadow cilial,
slopes of, beaded
musk of the well,
a far within un-
leashing seraph
primaries, forest-fire
pastels, a leaf,
hers, diapason.

PART TWO

Barcelona 99

Portrait

In a photo I possess
she's pink from the shower;
robe, cord, limbs converse;
towel-turbaned, damply she shines.

Odalisque, soubrette, chatelaine
(shortly to finger-dry hair),
she endows the fortunate chosen
with measured glee – 'Welcome

to *notre petit grenier* –
hideaway – trampoline –
dinner simmers – aperitif,
mon ami – or start with the wine?'

Accommodation

The walls, unabashed, thinned
to nothing as the building rose.
Not to damn them out of hand,
they served, upright, slanted,
scarred, fabulously singed.

A guard-dog lived next door.
It was this dog's habit to drive
at the shared wall, bark, murmur,
crackle sharps and flats of woe
whenever we made love,

our habit (agile, we sought
accommodation) to let him whirl
us thus into the salvatory straight,
past the blind post, post-
coital abatements and sprawl.

L'Aubergine

Nipples on deck, on fire,
to stroll Paris in the autumn
dusk, cunt composing this letter
to a mellifluous aubergine,

left hand the ribbon about his,
words such as *touchstone, heft,*
coming at you out of the trees,
is to be one with the drift

of bodies, spectators' attention,
clandestine buzz of shadow,
to meet – now – the woman
smiling, hand raised to slow

you, him, to say 'Beautiful
to see. Lovers. Stay a while.'

The Orange

The orange is not
the full shilling,
merely the skin,
whole and entire,

now it's a gourd
you might use as
float, rattle, par for
the with-it décor,

now a gourd-series,
gourd-head, torso,
gourd-arms, legs,
all in proportion,

heaven-sent heaven,
shy, breathless,
petite, horizontal,
all, all yours.

Wisps of Blue

To find the word
'plantureuse' waiting
as description will
do till some sweeter
bouquet comes along,

tells me it
means 'ample, copious,
lavish', remarks
'English doesn't cater
for what you are,'

has a way of allowing his tongue
discover the word
'plantureuse' you'd pay to record
or perhaps video,
arbitrary wisps of
blue departing
the eyes impregnate
aperçus, I can hear

them mutely singing
each to each
and wonder who
'si plantureuse' is
kissing him now?

Au Septième Étage

Spiral climb to
notre petit grenier

spiced slipstream in
which I tumble
lunging to slap
tip miss your un-
insurable cheeks

removed stairwell
absorbs the din

what floor are
we now love

such an ordinary
door of forest green
with Judas-hole
to spy unseen
open enter share
our ineluctable desired.

Bonheur d'Esclavage

Her panties not quite
dry shimmy in the hot
air-flow from the blower's
antic overdrive,

cream nothings, lace
somethings — *'Soit vite!'* — quiver,
hornpipe, foxtrot, hand
it to Bo Diddley,
Bo The Man

they couldn't put down —
'Ça va? Bien, très bien' —
we resume flight, spell
figures of eight (while
the blower rhymes
satisfaction), take off,
endeavour fresh lifts,
pirouettes, extensions,
demand an audition,
right now, at The Kirov …

October sun fills
our disordered lair,
the panties a pennant,
Bo Diddley and I
the breast of a linnet,
ma belle en retard,

brushing the hair,

ironing a blouse,
changing her shoes.

Ma Bouche Laiteuse

A photo I possess:
big, whoever she is,
for her age, boots,
prize panties, a
big girl now.

The *soupçon* of ruse;
and the brave mouth
sips ... what? *Lait.*
Ma bouche laiteuse,
where have you been?

He'll be home soon,
dinner, bistro till three,
the sack, lie late,
fuck till noon's
glazed afternoon.

Lancelot du Lac

Les contes de la lune vague
après la pluie has just gotta be
the finest movie ever made,

about love – what else? – and death,
full of mist above water, immodest
dissolves, departures, riddles
of return, houses separating plank
by plank to the sound of bells,
but what I remember most

are the lakes, paternoster and still.
You're a lake, I decided
that night, uncovered, *copain*,
you're a lake, mist plentiful,
a boat seen, lake again
(I monitor rapid eye motion).

Les contes de la lune vague
après la pluie – ghost people,
a woman, a man, the flame,
we came home, quiet, by water,
walking on water, the Seine, sister
canals, I thought, What the hell?
Is that a sheep or a pram? A
clochard shouted *'L'ectoplasma!'*

Mizoguchi directed it, and died –
so they say, o, decades back,
Mizoguchi's not dead, not a bit,

saw him attendant as we
meandered, looked like
Utamaro, Kawabata, the woman
who wrote that pillow-talk
book – or was she heathen Chinee?

My lake *copain*, mist,
boat seen, lake again.
The moon lay back on its tail,
Orion's belt only, the pair of us
telling over and over *Les contes
de la lune vague après la pluie* ...

Hansel

Butter her paws.

Butter one, butter all,
first fore, now hind,
pat for the tail,
pussy's on the mend.

Our dog next door
ripens his prehensile
fur. Time to admire
somebody's hansel.

The key of glass has a silver chain
and the equipoise
of donor unknown.

I caress the key,
deem it elegant.
The glass mists as we
breathe above it.

Thinking about Nothing

Odd time sails into my head,
'You've been on this giddy planet
thousand years more than good
for you, pet. Me. Whoever's next.'

Therefore, care for, why should anyone?
The hands, fair fucks, praise the hands.
Eyes, already, bequeathed to the nation.
The tongue'll always make amends.

My Little Prince Saint-Exupéry:
'Why can't I be somewhere else
since — look — I'm here anyway?'
An intake of breath that's caress.

I know it will vanish in tears.
Bright. Broken. Ours, love, ours.

Storytelling

From the start I told her stories,
from the start she listened,
now I was telling differently,
differently she'd listen.

You knew, you've always known,
pitch of the telling to be
contingent on the teller
heart hung out for daws
to sample, listener's alongside,
companion offertory, or,

as I recall, a hand,
brushing the teller, fashion
cantos to earn this hand
entirely composed of fine-
spun summer-scented hair.

Milk-White

A milk-white ear
listens to me, who
owns it, no idea,
who gave leave,
but, all stations,
it listens to me.

It arrived one day,
middle of the night,
settled in, behaved
more than smart
about most things,
for sure about me.

And can it talk
through the multiple lips?
Never yackety-yak,
chooses time, words,
sounds a note some-
where between benign
and The Windy Tree.
What does it say?
Says what the ghost-
Dad chiselled for me
that hour in the forest
of Seek-an'-Learn —

'Where's there's no flame,
pine for the burn.'

PART THREE

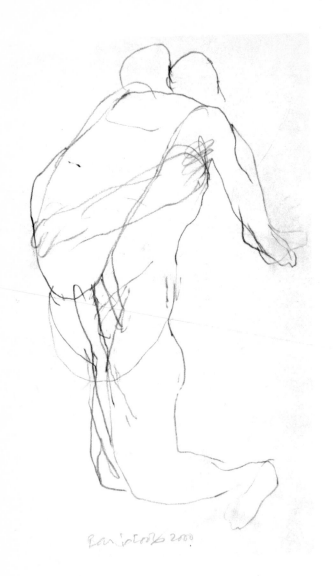

The Garden

I feel faintly Lilith,
recommend the experience.
We take it slow, up on
an hour to exhaustion.

'Seems we're unobserved,'
he laps my navel clean
of sweat. Unobserved.

Mark the day.
Our voyeur window's
here to stay.

The Party

She has just acknowledged
my eyes, proleptic, upon her.
'Complexion, high summer,
sonorous peaches-and-cream' –
he got that right, we look –
serenade – into each other,
into her, the inordinate side
of woman conjures acclaim
even at ninety, a hundred –
where's my drink? – whatever
ravine's this year the calendar.

    – Drumstick? Daiquiri? Devilled egg?
    – For my birthday, yes. Such a lug.

He's playing Sir Mostest, not
him at all, she's event
plus, what is it, the sap,
amaze, perilous, of knowing.
Could watch till I drop
(believe I'll sit down, sit).

    – The white's fine. Never touch red.
    Only bull's blood, as Joyce said.

I registered rapport, her eyes
move on, she'll tell him
before morning, weather of our
exchange, he'll say, 'I knew.'
My foot's numb. Where have you

gone, shy under the ash-
trays, anchovies, din, where,
blossom, where have you gone?

(The dancer idle by the door,
airy dewlap of red hair,
large white face, pastoral
rump, has of late won the title —
'Cows of Whites Eyes', not
to disparage the achievement.)

You've been invited here
to confirm a question.
Cordial, you have obliged.

Close-up

Not in your body,
lover-boy, any more?

Saw you rushed into
it other day, tho':
honest old Bewley's,
saw your children
step from the ground,
fill your limbs,
trunk, in one go.

'Blood jet' — *Voilà* —
as in Sylvia,

my face pressed
against the glass.

The Beast

She's never looked better. A ramble,
the populace admire, we match
stare for stare. The bold level
with us; second thought, touch
their shades. Ave, Jack. Hi, Jill.

Beast. The beast's bald, bull-head,
flaccid receding snout, uniform
off-white bar pale red
eyes that, reined tight, roam.

Behold her advance, engage the bull-
head, small-talk the owner.
The beast is dog, warms to her
animal affections. Both are well.
Corpsed actor ingests the marvel.

The Manifest

Svelte lips
of the true Gael;

deviant septum,
unmissable;

far-from-home
stalled eyes.

What is it about Ireland?
'The soil', he said, 'burns.'

A Certain Room

Is it true
that in a certain
room of the castle we always
love the once beloved?

Where's that room?
On the seventh floor!

Once a lifetime,
you may by accident
or prayer or unsolicited gift
discover it,

shed the maze,
astonished stand.
Everything as was.
And more. And more.

Directions

You went north
where the birds
know too much
and the stones
rise early.

Blackbird of Inishowen,
ordinary phantom,
time and again
persuaded worm
from earth, held
worm aloft, gulped.

Carndonagh's Christian
remains: your hand sped,
unknowing, to the fish-
flicker in the upright's
ravaged side.

Post-bellum

Turned the corner,
you're on the next street,
could be Neptune.

The current, a lamb,
examines me in fret.

'I blush,' out
it comes, 'therefore I am.'
Watch his eyes hunt.

Au Lit

Bed I wanted
(before you came)
to drown in snow —

Floor-mattress, twi-
lit corner of
the *petit grenier* —

That haunted bed
where we might
not make love —

The one — king-size —
destined to see us out —

Awoke, fragrance
beside me, morning
after you left,
drew another breath,
lay there years.